3, 2, 1...
DRAW!

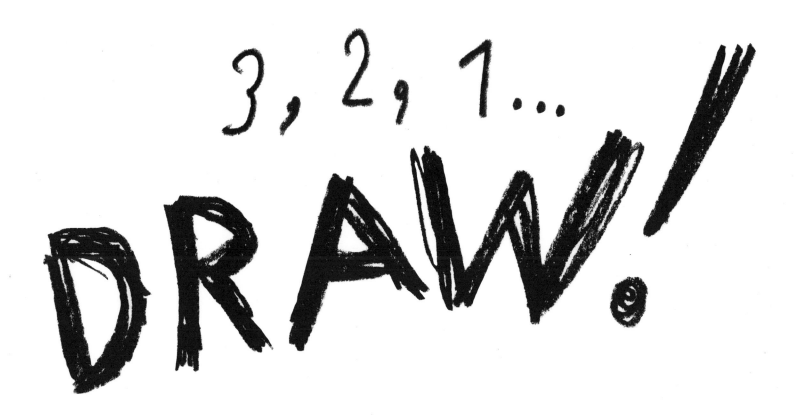

SERGE BLOCH

WIDE EYED EDITIONS

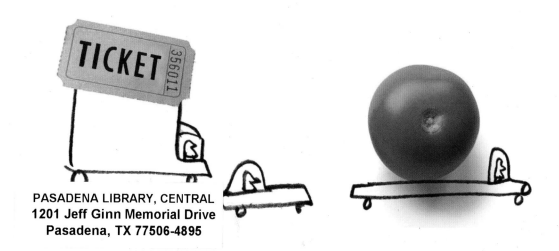

TRANSFORM YOUR KITCHEN

Sniff
Sniff

Grumph.

What is this eggplant saying?

How many other creatures are hiding in Asparagus Forest?

Can you name these pan-bots?

Create your own pan-vention.

Hello!

Meet the Spork Family.

Bring some life to this knife, spoon, and fork.

A cupful of love . . .

What's the story here?

Add some snails to this trail.

Create your own big cheese.

Bring this roll to life.

TRANSFORM YOUR LIVING ROOM

Who else is in the hot seat?

What other telephone transformations are taking place?

Who is making a spectacle of themselves?

Design your own apartment blocks.

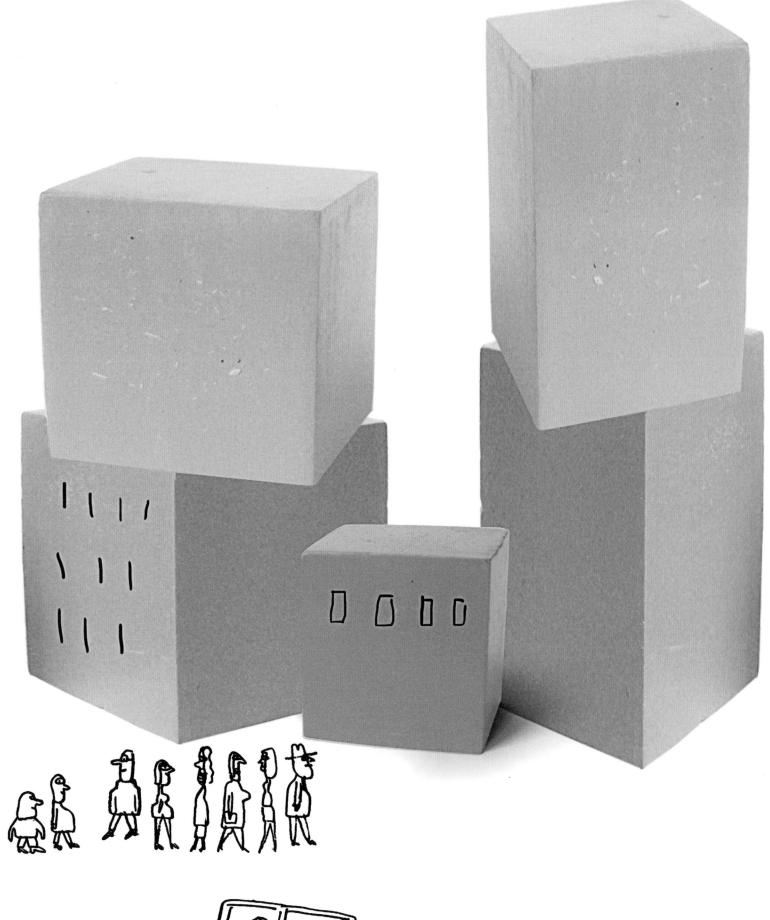

What message would
you like to send?

Who is in a jam?

What other characters
are getting keyed up?

Who is the strongest of them all?

TRANSFORM YOUR BEDROOM

Who is under each of these hats?

Give each bear a belly.

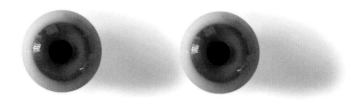

Who else is keeping an eye on things?

What has set the alarm bells ringing?

Create some covers.

Who else has slipped into a slipper?

What is lurking among these lamps?

TRANSFORM YOUR BATHROOM

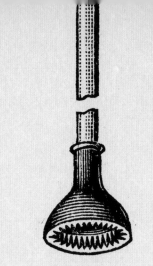

Who will not be brushed aside?

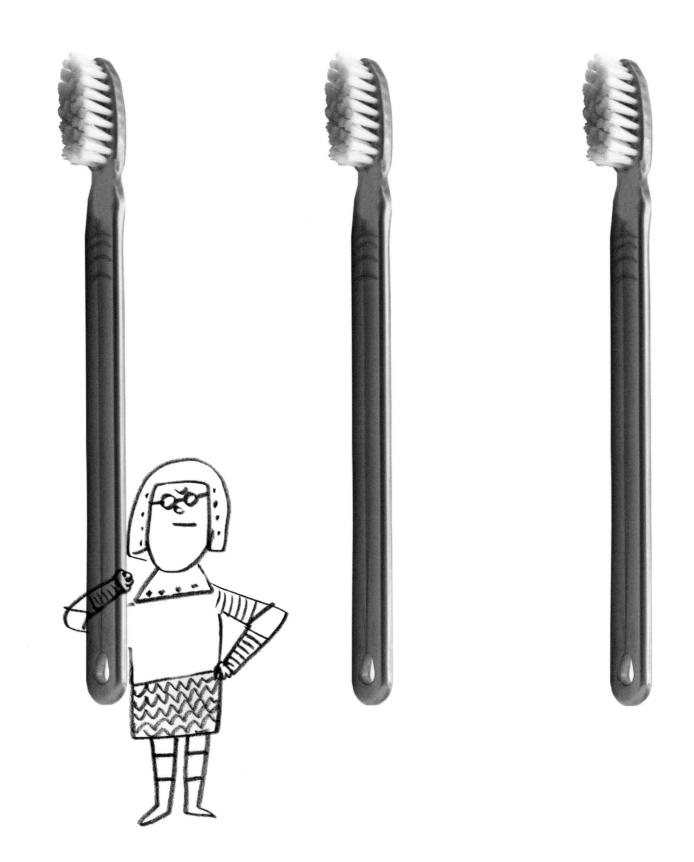

Draw some more seafarer's stories.

What is flying through these clouds of cotton?

Who's a lucky duck?

What other faucet friends have you found?

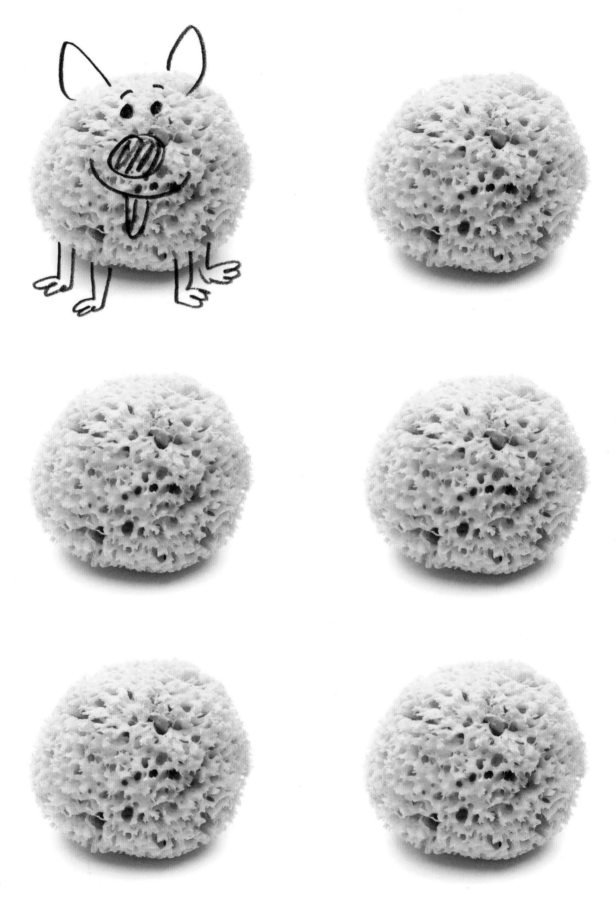

Draw some more squeaky-clean creatures.

Mirror, mirror, on the wall, can you fill these pictures, all?

Who is in this toilet paper caper?

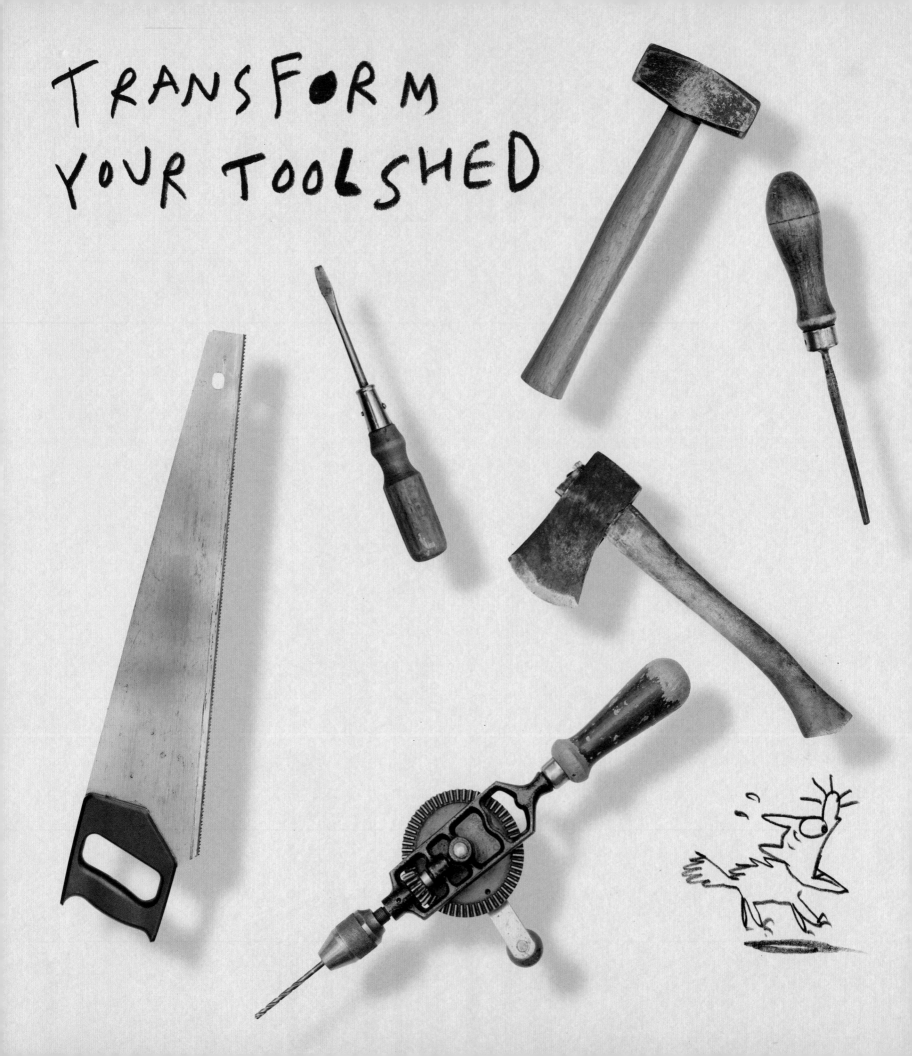

Bring your own inventions to light.

Who—or what—is feeling red-faced?

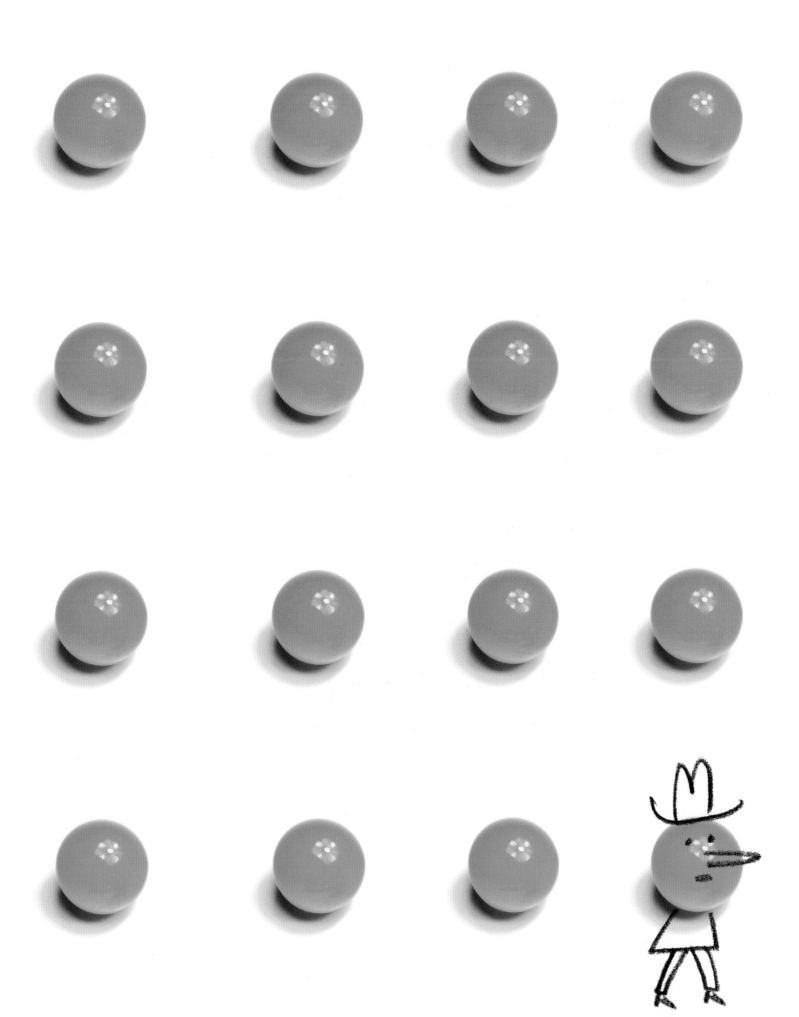

FIRE FIRE!

Who else is coming to the rescue?

Who is pulling on this string?

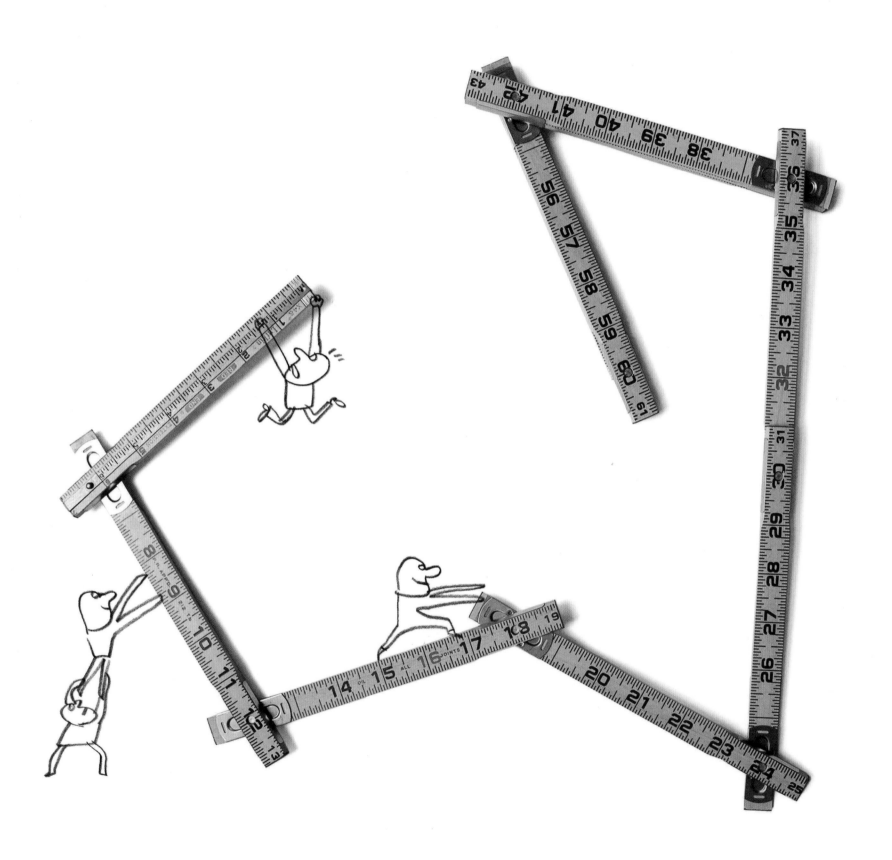

Who is ruling the roost?

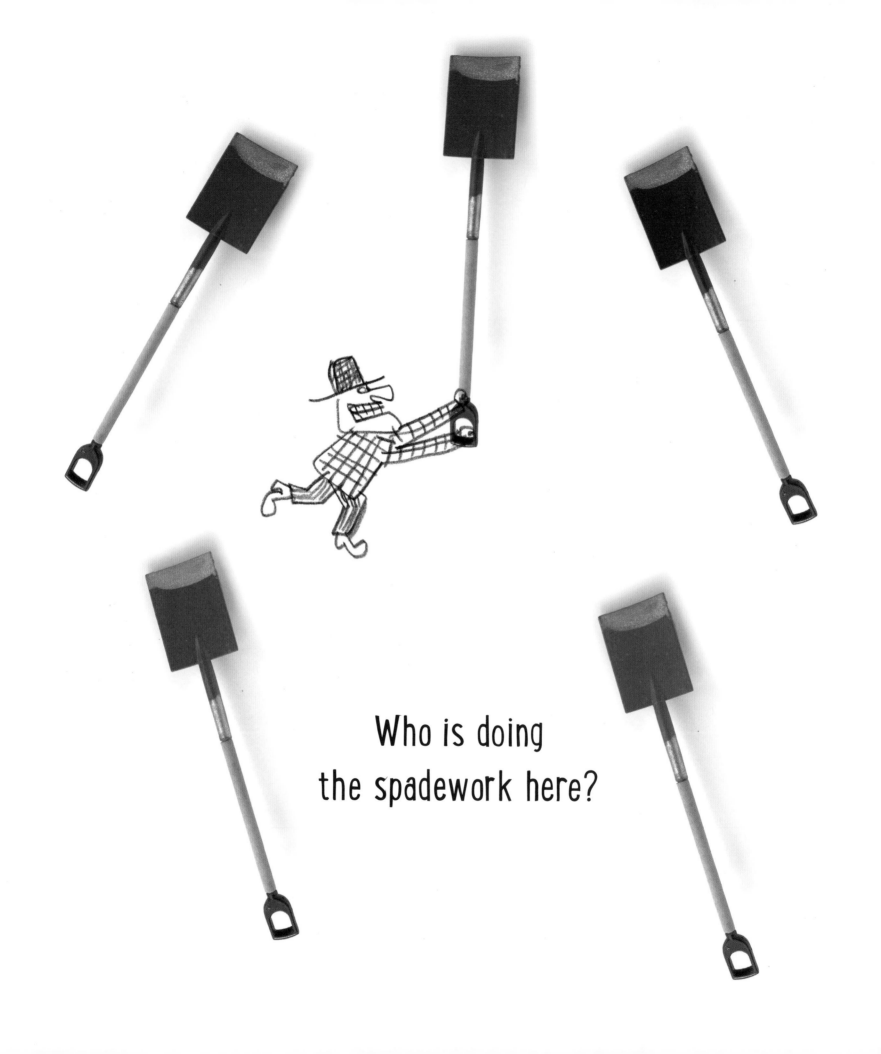

Who is doing
the spadework here?

What can the saw-player see?

TRANSFORM YOUR BACKYARD

Add some feathered
friends hiding in
these branches.

Who else is having a prickly conversation?

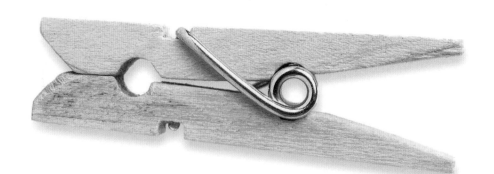

Create some more clothespin creatures . . .

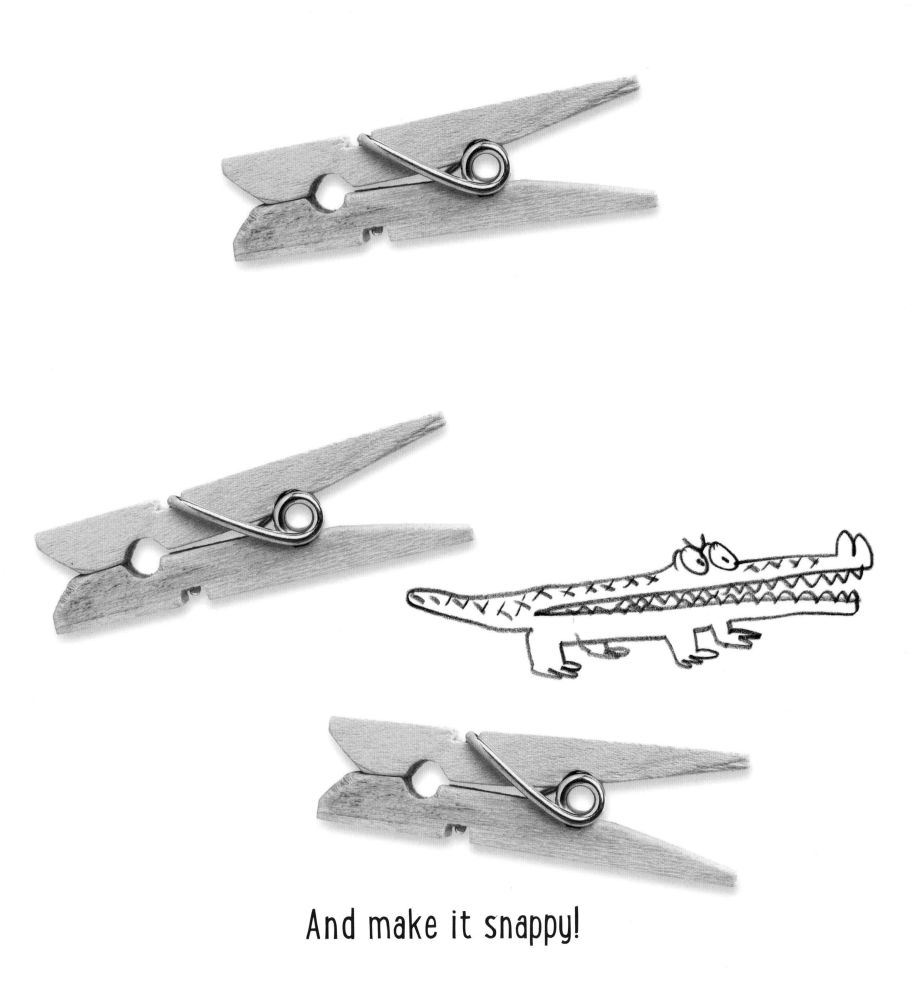

And make it snappy!

Add some
flower power.

Create a crew of conker-ers!

Who is ready to fly the nest?

Create your own
can of worms.

Wide Eyed Editions
www.wideeyededitions.com

3,2,1, Draw! copyright © Aurum Press Ltd 2016
Illustrations copyright © Serge Bloch 2016

First published in the United States in 2016 by Wide Eyed Editions
an imprint of Quarto Inc.,
276 Fifth Avenue, Suite 206, New York, NY 10001.
www.wideeyededitions.com

ISBN 978-1-84780-774-8

The illustrations were created with mixed media
Set in Lunchbox

Designed by Nicola Price
Edited by Jenny Broom and Harriet Balfour Evans
Published by Rachel Williams

Printed in China

1 3 5 7 9 8 6 4 2